ANIMALS
That Make a Difference!

Giraffes

Ashley Lee

Explore other books at:
WWW.ENGAGEBOOKS.COM

VANCOUVER, B.C.

℮ → WWW.ENGAGEBOOKS.COM

Giraffes: Pre-1
Animals That Make a Difference!
Lee, Ashley, 1995
Text © 2025 Engage Books
Design © 2025 Engage Books

Edited by: A.R. Roumanis, and Ashley Lee
Design by: Mandy Christiansen

Text set in Arial Regular.

FIRST EDITION / FIRST PRINTING

library and archives canada cataloguing in publication

Title: Giraffes / Ashley Lee.
Names: Lee, Ashley, author.
Description: Series statement: Animals that make a difference

Identifiers: Canadiana (print) 20230448542 | Canadiana (ebook) 20230448569
ISBN 978-1-77878-687-7 (hardcover)
ISBN 978-1-77878-696-9 (softcover)

Subjects:
LCSH: Giraffes—Juvenile literature.
LCSH: Human-animal relationships—Juvenile literature.

Classification: LCC QL737.P94 C38 2025 | DDC J599.885—DC23

This project has been made possible in part by the Government of Canada.

Canada

Look up!

3

Giraffes are the tallest land animal.

4

They are taller
than some houses!

Giraffes have small bumps on their heads.

6

Their bodies have lots of spots.

Giraffes live in grasslands in Africa.

They live in groups called herds.

9

Wild giraffes only sleep for about 30 minutes each day.

Giraffes hum to
each other at night.

12

People are not sure why they do this.

13

Giraffes have very long tongues.

They are able to grab food with them.

15

Giraffes eat leaves.

Their favorite are acacia (uh-KAY-shuh) leaves.

Giraffes eat from the tops of trees.

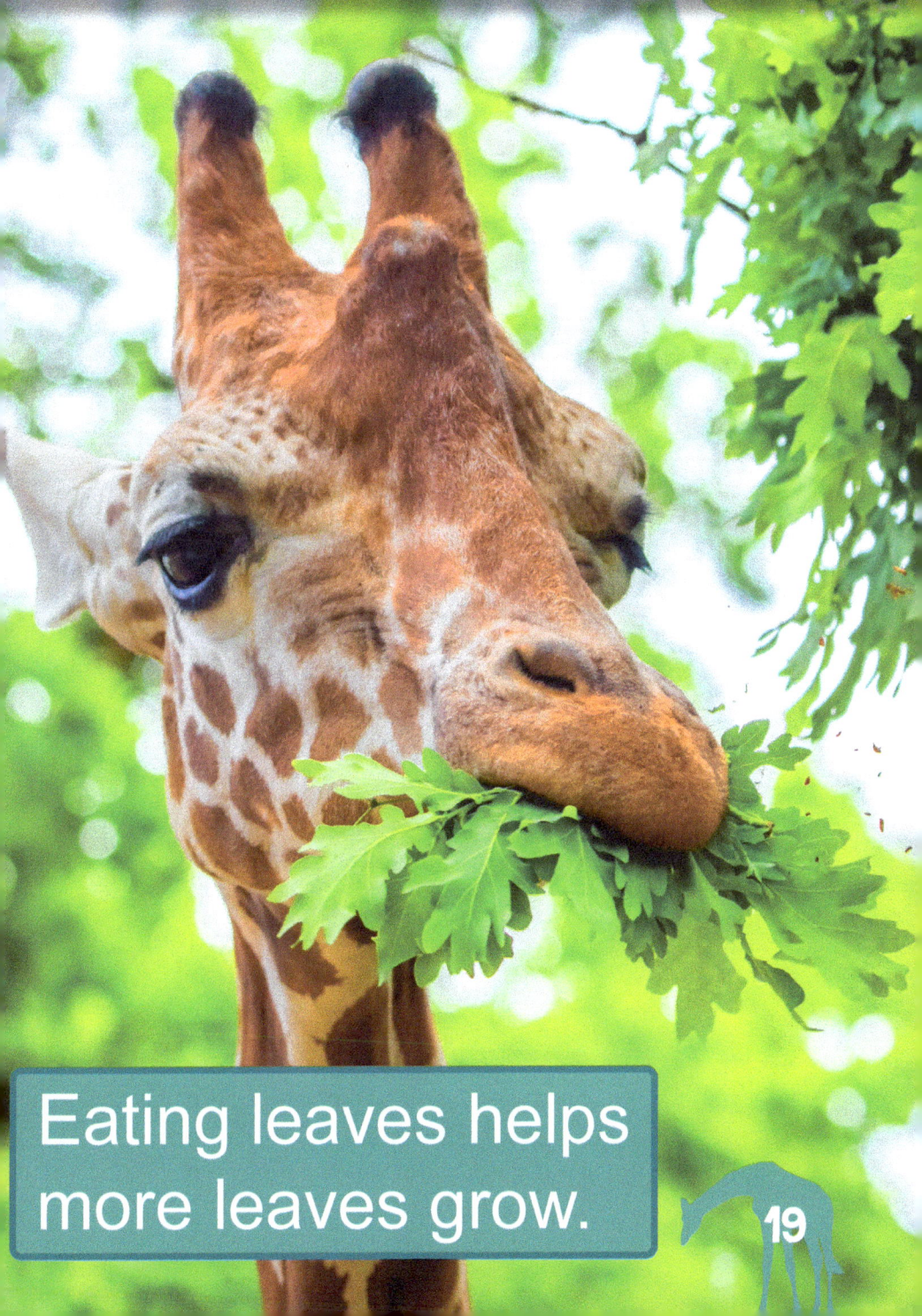

Eating leaves helps more leaves grow.

Giraffes eat seeds
when they eat leaves.

These seeds come out in their poop.

Giraffe poop helps the seeds grow.

It helps plants
stay healthy.

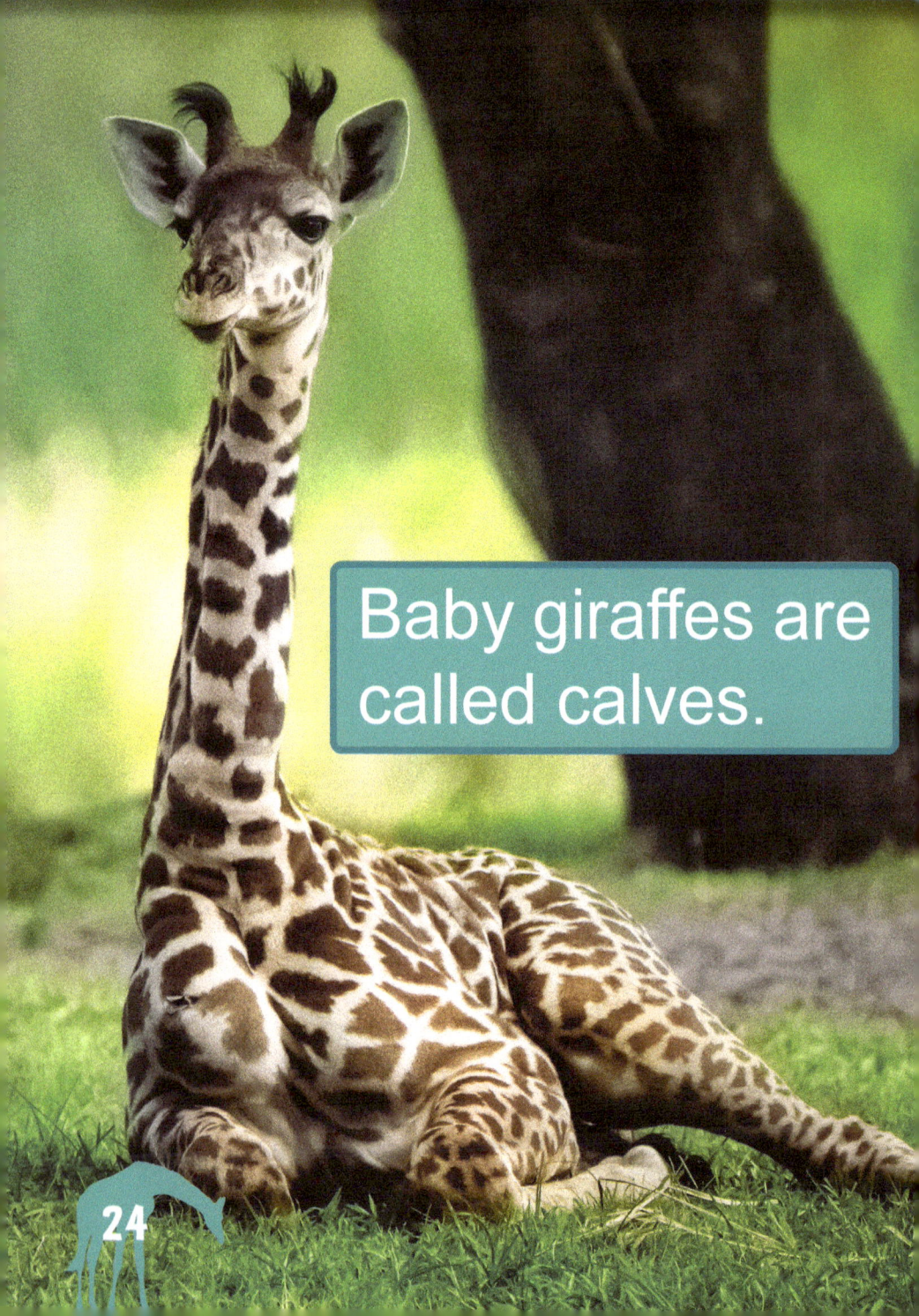

Baby giraffes are called calves.

Giraffes have one calf at a time.

Giraffes give
birth standing up.

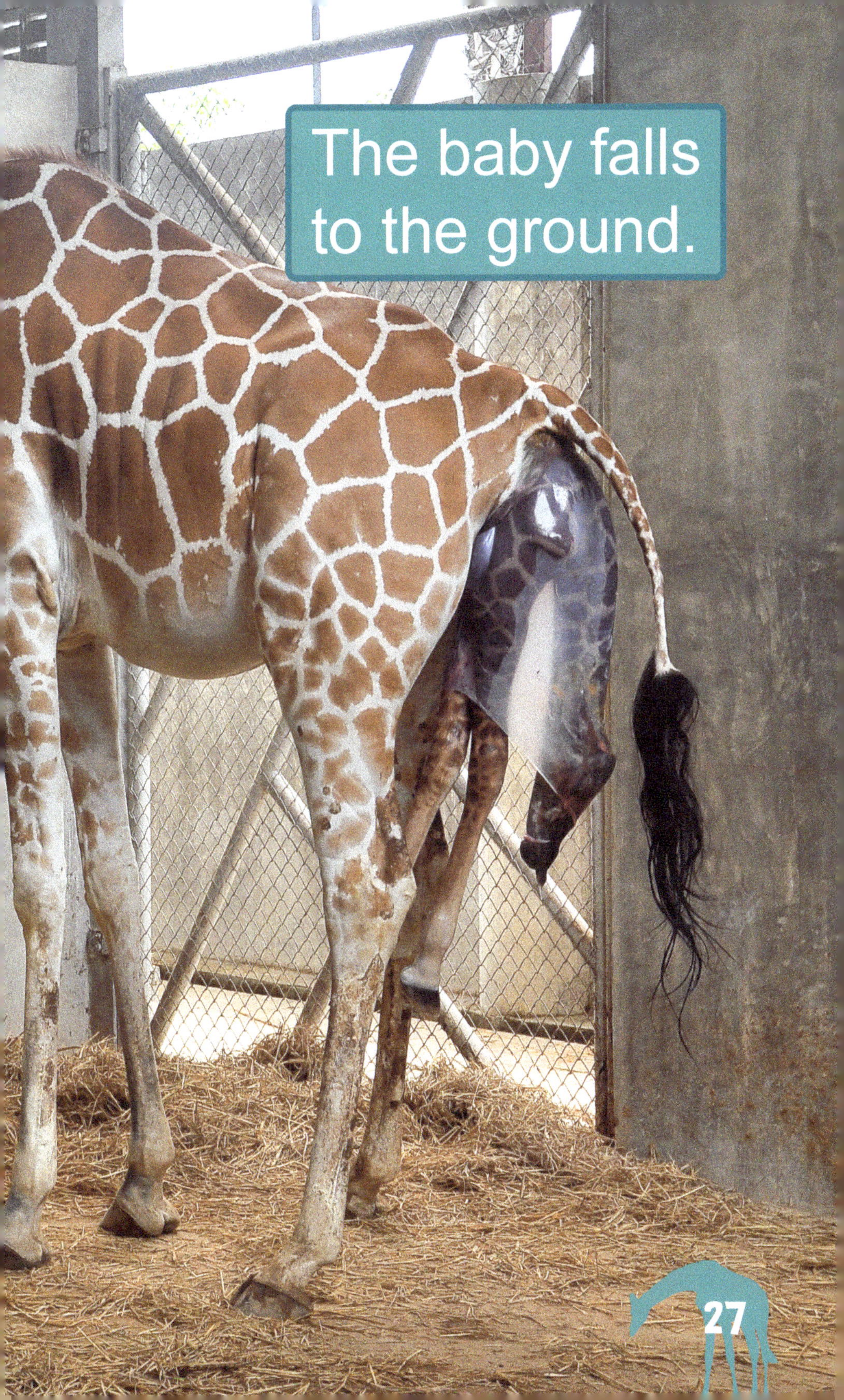

The baby falls to the ground.

Baby giraffes can stand 30 minutes after birth.

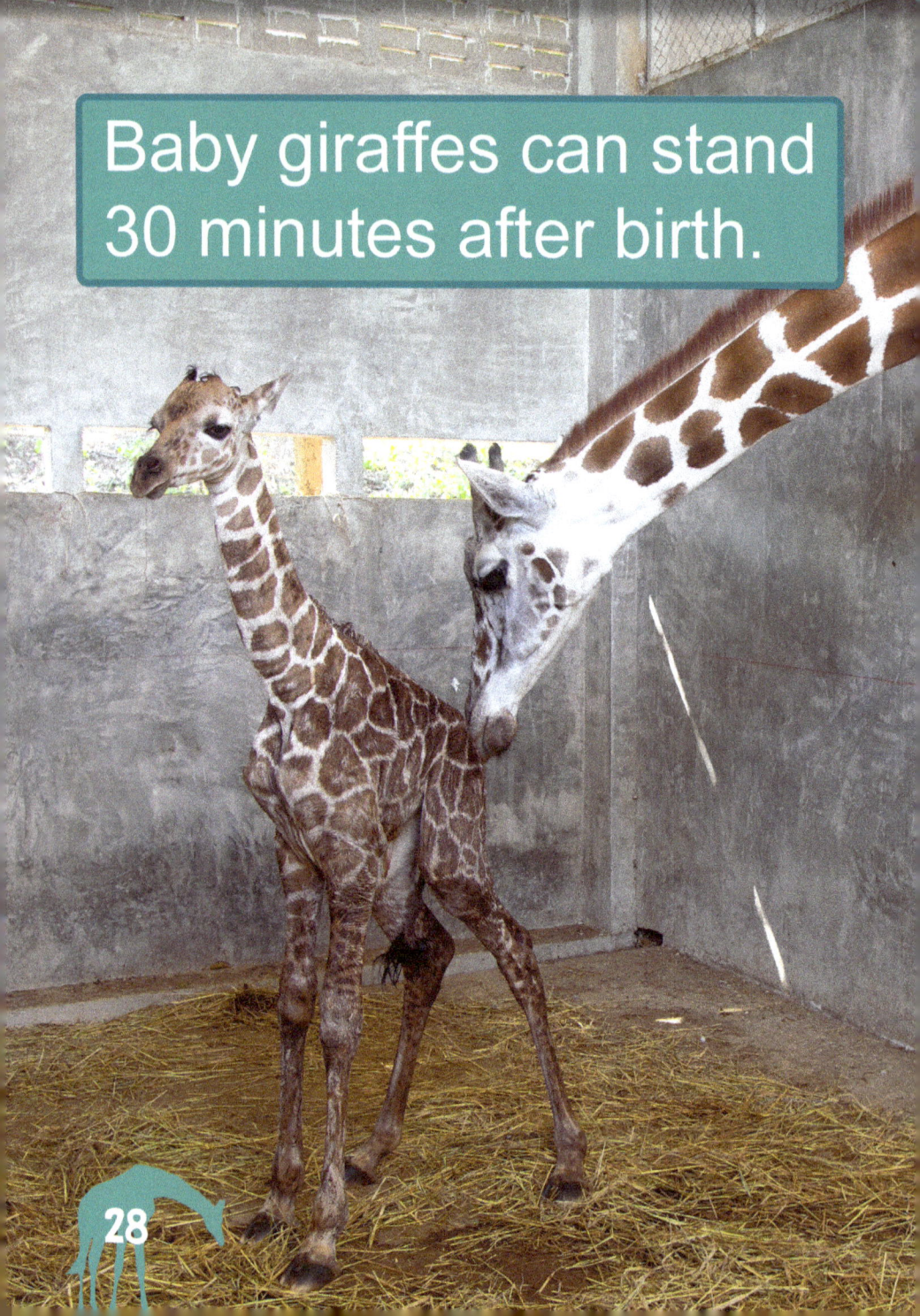

They live for
about 20 years.

29

Quiz

Test your knowledge of giraffes by answering the following questions. The questions are based on what you have read in this book. The answers are listed on the bottom of the next page.

1 Are giraffes the tallest land animal?

2 Do giraffes have small bumps on their heads?

3 Do giraffes eat leaves?

4 Does giraffe poop help seeds grow?

5 Are baby giraffes called calves?

6 Do giraffes live for about 20 years?

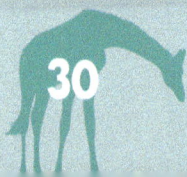

Explore other books in the
Animals That Make a Difference series

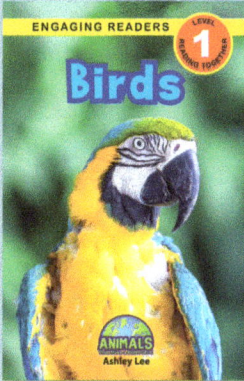

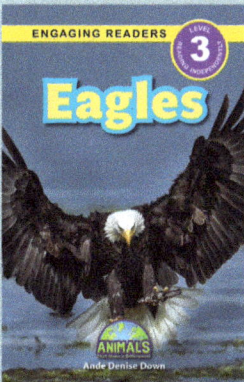

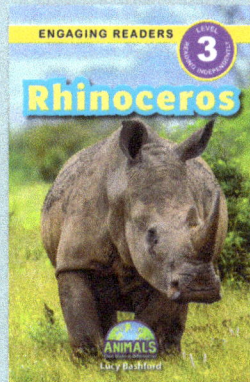

ENGAGING READERS — LEVEL 1 — READING TOGETHER
Birds
Ashley Lee

ENGAGING READERS — LEVEL 1 — READING TOGETHER
Ladybugs
Ashley Lee

ENGAGING READERS — LEVEL 1 — READING TOGETHER
Squirrels
Ashley Lee

ENGAGING READERS — LEVEL 2 — READING WITH HELP
Butterflies
Ashley Lee

ENGAGING READERS — LEVEL 2 — READING WITH HELP
Frogs
Ashley Lee

ENGAGING READERS — LEVEL 2 — READING WITH HELP
Octopuses
Ashley Lee

ENGAGING READERS — LEVEL 3 — READING INDEPENDENTLY
Eagles
Ande Denise Down

ENGAGING READERS — LEVEL 3 — READING INDEPENDENTLY
Ravens
AJ Knight

ENGAGING READERS — LEVEL 3 — READING INDEPENDENTLY
Rhinoceros
Lucy Bashford

Visit www.engagebooks.com to explore more Engaging Readers.

Answers:
1. Yes 2. Yes 3. Yes 4. Yes 5. Yes 6. Yes

www.ingramcontent.com/pod-product-compliance
Lightning Source LLC
Chambersburg PA
CBHW052035030426
42337CB00027B/5019